morn - ing stars are__ ris - ing,_____ bright__ morn - ing stars are__

morn - ing stars are ris - ing,_____ bright__ morn - ing stars are__

Bright__ morn - ing stars_____ ris - ing, morn - ing stars are__

Bright__ morn - ing stars_____ ris - ing, morn - ing stars are__

ris - ing,__ bright__ morn - ing stars are__ ris - ing._____ Day__

ris - ing,__ bright__ morn - ing stars are ris - ing._____ Day__

ris - ing,__ bright__ morn - ing stars_____ ris - ing. Day__

ris - ing,__ bright__ morn - ing stars_____ ris - ing. Day__

for Sarah Hendry

2. Little wheel a-turnin'

Trad.
arr. **MICHAEL HIGGINS**

10

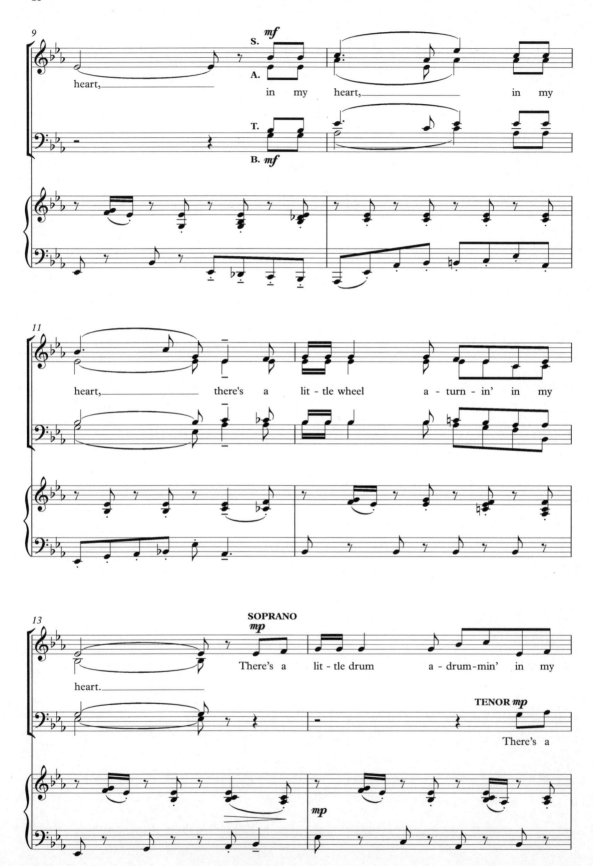

lit - tle song a - sing - in' in my heart,_____ in my

heart,_____ in my heart,_____ there's a

lit - tle song a - sing - in' in my heart,_____ in my

for Caleb Pillsbury

3. He's gone away

Trad., from North Carolina
arr. **MICHAEL HIGGINS**

X791   Three American Songs   HIGGINS

ISBN 978-0-19-354051-4